WHAT WALL STREET WON'T TELL YOU

RYAN JONES

Disclaimer

All information in this is book is based on my experience and study over the last decade. None of this material should be taken as investment advice. All investments entail risk, and any investment actions or decisions that you make, as a result of any information contained in this book, are your sole responsibility.

ISBN: 0615475116
ISBN-13: 9780615475110
Library of Congress Control Number: 2011905800

**What Wall Street Won't Tell You:
A Guide to Personal Finance and Investing**

By Ryan Jones

ACKNOWLEDGEMENTS

I would like to thank everyone who has supported me throughout the years. First are my parents. Dad, you are my best friend and my hero. You have always been there to provide wise advice, even when I didn't want to listen. Mom, you have always been there to tell me how wonderful I am, even when I wasn't too wonderful. I love you both very much.

To Lauren, you are the sunshine in my life. You are the one who brings the light to my life every day. You make me realize that every day is a gift, especially when I can spend it with you. You embrace my quirks when no one else does. Thank you for supporting me and all of my wild ideas.

To Jennifer, thank you for putting up with me. I am sure it was not always easy to have me as a big brother. I really appreciate your optimism and support throughout the years. Your happiness is contagious, and I couldn't ask for a better sister.

Justin, you are the best brother-in-law I could ask for. Thank you for all of the conversations and advice throughout the years. I look forward to many more in the coming decades. Thanks for everything you have done for me over the years.

To Leroy, Marianne, Helen, and Orville, you were wonderful grandparents. I miss you all. Thank you for the love and support that you gave me while you were here. I am grateful for the time I was able to spend with you all.

To all of the friends who have stuck by me throughout the years, thank you. Special thanks go to Preston, William, and Scott. You are like brothers to me. You are always there to listen when I call. We can go months without speaking, and when we do, it is like we never skipped a beat.

To Jordan, I miss you and love you. My goal every day is to live life as you lived it. You taught me what love was and that every moment is to be cherished. You are always with me. To Sam, Chom, and Bailey, I miss you guys, too. I am glad to have had each of you in my life, even if it was just for a short time. To Jake, you make me laugh every day. You are always there to make me feel important. I love you, buddy.

To anyone that I may have left out, thank you for your help and support throughout the years. There are too many to name. It has been a long journey to this point, and there have been many who have helped me get to this point in my life. Thank you to you all.

TABLE OF CONTENTS

REFERENCES

1. "12 Warning Signs of U.S. Hyperinflation," *Inflation.us*. National Inflation Association, 2011. 26 March 2011. http://inflation.us/ hyperinflationwarningsigns.html.

2. "World Population: 1950-2050." *Census. gov*. U.S. Census Bureau, 2011. 23 February 2011. http://www.census.gov/ipc/www/idb/ worldpopgraph.php.

3. "Monthly Historical Money Stock Tables: Components of Non-M1 M2 (SA)." *Federalreserve.gov*. U.S. Federal Reserve, 2011. 24 March 2011. http://www.federalreserve.gov/ release/h6/hist/h6hist3.pdf.

4. "2007 Census of Agriculture: Farmers by Age." *Usda.gov*. USDA, 2009. 4 February 2009. http://www.agcensus.usda.gov/ Publications/2007/Online_Highlights/Fact_ Sheets/farmer_age.pdf.

5. "Summary of Receipts, Outlays, and Surpluses or Deficits." *Whitehouse.gov*. United States White House, 2011. 14 February 2011. http://www. whitehouse.gov/omb/budget/Historicals/.

6. "The Debt to the Penny and Who Holds it."
    Treasurydirect.gov. U.S. Treasury, 2011. 31 March
    2011. http://www.treasurydirect.gov/NP/
    BPDLogin?application=np.

7. "Interest Expense on the Debt Outstanding."
    Treasurydirect.gov. U.S. Treasury, 2011. 4 March
    2011. http://www.treasurydirect.gov/govt/
    reports/ir/ir_expense.htm.

8. "Major Foreign Holders of Treasury Securities."
    Treasury.gov. U.S. Treasury, 2011. 15 March
    2011. http://www.treasury.gov/resource-
    center/data-chart-center/tic/Documents/mfh.
    txt.

9. "Ownership of Federal Securities: Table OFS-
    2. – Estimated Ownership of U.S. Treasury
    Securities." *Treasury.gov.* U.S. Treasury, 2011.
    15 March 2011. http://fms.treas.gov/bulletin/
    index.html.

10. Faith, Curtis M. *Way of the Turtle.* (New York,
    NY: McGraw-Hill, 2007).

RESOURCES

1. www.Auction.com – Resource for online real estate auctions.

2. www.Mint.com – Resource for tracking all of your personal finances in one place.

3. www.bgeneral.com – Bank in Panama that currently allows US citizens to open accounts.

4. www.inflation.us – National Inflation Association website for information on economic research.

5. www.grahaminvestor.com – Great tool for generating a list of stocks that are trading under their current estimated intrinsic value.

6. Finance.yahoo.com – Great overall investment site for tracking stock prices, finding values of companies, such as Enterprise Value and EBITDA, and keeping up with financial news.

"Until one is committed, there is always hesitancy, the chance to draw back, always ineffectiveness. Concerning all acts of initiative (and creation), there is one elementary truth, the ignorance of which kills countless ideas and splendid plans: that the moment one definitely commits oneself, then providence moves too. Whatever you can do, or dream you can, begin it. Boldness has genius, power, and magic in it."

—J. W. von Goethe

INTRODUCTION

The purpose of this book is to share with you everything I have learned that Wall Street doesn't share with the average investor. My aim is to break everything down in terms that everyone can understand. Wall Street makes it difficult, if not impossible, for the average investor to understand. This is a shame, since money and how we use it is something that affects nearly every person in the world.

This book represents a compilation of all that I have learned over the last ten years of pouring myself into learning what I could about personal finance and investing. It is based on my studies, successes, and failures. I will lay it all out for you to see. My goal is to pass along the knowledge I wish someone had given to me ten years ago, when I was first starting out.

I have a bachelor's degree in mechanical engineering, a MBA in general business from Troy State University, and a MBA in finance from Emory

University. I know—two MBAs—I am a glutton for punishment. Along with the formal degrees, I have countless hours of trading experience; I have read hundreds of finance books and thousands of finance articles. I also run a finance-related blog and manage a fund for my own money, but we will get to that later.

In 2001, I graduated from Auburn University with a degree in mechanical engineering. I really had no interest in engineering, but I was good at math, and my family had always worked for the power company. I had no idea what I wanted to do with my life, so I figured I would just study engineering, get a job, and figure it all out later.

After graduation, the economy tanked, and then 9/11 happened. I finally found work with a packaging company as a design engineer. The plant where I went to work closed within a year of my start date, and I was transferred to a plant in South Carolina.

Little did I know, shortly after moving to South Carolina, I would discover the passion that would shape the rest of my life. I have been chasing this passion ever since. This passion is investing and making money grow.

Chapter 1

~ STORY OF PASSION ~

Like most other people, I was never taught a lot about money or investing in school. There were probably a few lessons on interest growth in my college finance course but never anything that really taught me how to use money, save it, and invest it properly. I guess it is just assumed that people will figure these things out on their own.

Even after working part-time jobs for several years and one full year at my first full-time job, I didn't know how to handle money. The only thing I knew was to put as much as I could into my savings account and to pay off my debts as soon as I could. I knew that credit cards were bad, but I had no idea why. I had only had one loan, which my dad co-signed with me for a car. The thought of investments and buying stocks terrified me. I thought that was some magical area for people who had knowledge that I would never have.

My eyes were opened early in 2001, when my dad casually mentioned that he had just bought some

HealthSouth stock, and it was selling for just a few pennies per share. I knew of HealthSouth because it was a huge company in Alabama, and several people I knew even worked there. I had never had a brokerage account, but I knew that this was a good opportunity.

I convinced my dad to buy me a thousand shares, while I opened my own brokerage account and deposit money into it. He was able to purchase those shares for me at 28¢ per share. Later that year, I sold those shares at $6.50 per share.

I had made $6500 on an investment of $280! I was hooked. I thought this investing stuff was easy—boy was I wrong! All I could think about was investing. I immediately started buying other stocks and trying to learn as much as I could.

At the time, I was working on my MBA from Troy State University, but they did not offer any classes on investing—just the basic finance courses. There was no way this was going to teach me everything I needed to know. I read every article I could find on investing. I read investing books. I talked to everyone I knew about investing. I just wanted to absorb as much knowledge as I could, as quickly as I could. Little did I now that this was going to be a long journey that would require thousands of hours of reading, studying, and hands-on experience. I would go on to lose that $6500, plus a lot more, as

I tried seemingly every strategy known to man to extract a few dollars from the markets.

Over the last ten years, I have read books on value stocks, growth stocks, distressed debt, international investing, and commodities. I have read biographies of famous investors, books on the real estate collapse, personal finance, leadership principles, and success principles. More than anything, I wanted to learn how to get rich, and I studied everything I thought might give me an idea of how to get there. The problem was, I wanted it quick and I was ignoring the basic building blocks of investing.

After a few years of trying to learn it on my own, I decided that I should go to school to learn from people who could teach me how to invest and could help me to get a job on Wall Street. This would prove to be an expensive lesson.

I enrolled in Emory University's Goizueta Business School in August of 2007. I just knew that going to a top twenty-five business school would be the missing key that would get me to my goal. During my three years, I did learn a lot about balance sheets, income statements, cash flow statements, and many other subjects that would ultimately prove useful, as I moved along the path towards becoming a great investor.

There was one thing missing—no one was there who could teach me how to be a successful investor. They certainly gave me the tools to evaluate investments, but they did not teach me the secrets of investing.

I was thankful that I was getting close to putting together everything I had learned over the previous ten years. This is really not surprising since study after study has shown that it typically takes ten years of deep, concentrated study to get really good at any endeavor.

With that in mind, over the next nine chapters I am going to lay out everything I have learned in terms that almost anyone can grasp. I am going to pull back the curtain to reveal how to manage your money successfully and how to help you become comfortable with your personal finances and investing your money.

My goal is to help you understand the principles that took me ten years to discover and put into usable form. I hope you will be able to use these principles to take control of your own financial life, whether that means investing money for the long term, saving money for a new house, or getting out of debt. It is up to you to take these principles and make them your own. We will cover personal finance, economics, valuing businesses, selecting stocks, commodities, gold and silver, bonds, speculation, and putting it all together in a model portfolio. Let's get started!

Chapter 2

~ **PERSONAL FINANCE** ~

Personal finance is something that every one of us should be taught from a very early age. The exact age is debatable and probably different for each one of us, but we should certainly be taught personal finance, beginning in middle school. This should be a mandatory subject for every student from sixth grade, right up through college, regardless of major.

We are all required to take basic math, language, science, and history classes, yet none of us is ever taught about money. This is an awful injustice to every person alive today. If the basics of personal finance and money handling were taught in schools, we would have far fewer people in personal financial difficulties, and I would go so far as to say that our country would be in better financial shape, as well. So, what are the basics of personal finance that each of us should be taught?

The main concepts that should be taught are balancing a checkbook, the dangers of credit-card debt, the impact and real cost of interest on loans, and saving a portion of your pay for the future. If just these four basic concepts were taught in school, people would be more financially secure, and I would daresay much happier. Personal finance issues cause many of the personal and relationship problems that we see today. From couples getting divorced because of financial difficulty to unnecessary bankruptcies, personal financial issues cause deep pain and stress to the average person.

So, let's tackle these issues, here, and lay out a plan for your financial success. We will work through the following issues:

- Setting up a monthly budget
- Structuring and eliminating debt
- Determining which items can be borrowed for
- Establishing a savings plan
- Establishing an investment/cash-generation plan
- Enjoying your money

This looks like a lot of information to cover, but you will soon see that it can all be put together easily into an easy-to-follow plan, just by following a few simple rules.

Setting Up a Monthly Budget

Setting up a monthly budget can be as simple or as difficult as we want to make it. The very first step you should take is to determine how much money you bring home (take home pay) each month. From there, you can determine where it goes each month. After you determine how much money you have each month, you should look at your current bills. What bills do you have? If you are like most people you will have at least these:

- Mortgage/Rent
- Groceries
- Power
- Telephone
- Car Payment
- Insurance
- Cable/Internet
- Consumer Debt/Student Loans
- Gas

After you pay these bills each month, your goal is to have something left over for savings, investments, and fun money. Let's concentrate on just paying the bills, for now. There are some basic rules you should put into place for these bills as a part of your income. The first and major rule is how much house should we be paying for? I would tend to say that 35 percent of take-home pay is the maximum that should be put towards housing each month.

That leaves you with 65 percent of your take-home pay to spread across all of the other areas in your financial universe each month.

Your car payment should be no more than 15 percent of your take home pay. We would prefer not to have a car payment, but we will address that in the debt-elimination section a little later on. Allowing 15 percent for your car payment and 35 percent for your house payment has already consumed 50 percent of your take-home pay. Now, you have to figure out how to live on the rest of your money.

Groceries is an area where you can cut some corners by using a rewards card at your grocery store, buying items that are on sale, and cutting coupons each week. There are actually websites now that provide manufacturers' coupons, as well as store coupons. A quick Internet search yields several sites that provide this service for free.

Power, telephone, cable/Internet, and insurance should all be bills that are somewhat fixed each month. There are some good ways to cut these costs, as well. You can cut your power bill by shopping rates from energy companies if that is an option in your area, especially natural gas companies. I recently saved over 40 percent per month just by calling my current natural gas provider and informing them of an offer I received in the mail from one of their competitors. Eliminating extras such as DVR and premium channels from the cable plan can reduce Cable/Internet costs. You can further reduce the cost by eliminating cable television altogether and taking advantage of the growing television offerings on sites such as fancast.com and hulu.com. Insurance costs can also be reduced by shopping your insurance provider against competitors. This should probably be done once a year, just to make sure that you are receiving the best prices.

Gas prices will continue to fluctuate. This is an unfortunate situation that we cannot easily control. There are some things you can do to reduce these costs. You can walk or ride a bike to places close to your home, such as a nearby store or restaurant. You can carpool with coworkers who live near you. You can also take public transportation, as much as is convenient for you. One thing you should never do is go out and buy a more fuel-efficient car, just for the sake of saving money on gas. If you need to buy a new car, anyway, then go ahead and get the fuel-efficient model, but buying a new car just to save gas money is never financially advantageous.

Let's look at an example. Say you drive 20,000 miles per year in your current car, and that car gets 20 mpg. That is a thousand gallons of gas that you purchase every year. If the current cost of gas is $3 per gallon that is a total cost of $3000 per year for gas. Suddenly, gas prices double to $6 per gallon, and your new cost per year for gas is $6000. Now, let's say you buy a new car for $15,000. The new car gets 40 mpg, so you now only have to pay the original $3000 per year for gas. (That is 500 gallons times $6 per gallon.) So you saved $3000 per year on gas. It will take you five years of saving $3000 on gas per year before you break even on the $15,000 purchase of the new car. So you can see that it is not a good idea to buy a new car just to save money on gas.

Finally, we have our consumer/student loan debt. The target for this column is zero percent. I understand that, sometimes, emergencies happen, and you need to make a credit-card purchase. This should only be done in emergencies. Some people say that they like to use credit cards for the benefits and that they pay them off each month. I have found that this is typically an excuse, and the credit cards don't get paid off each month. With the top credit-card rates currently at 59.9 percent, no amount of points in the world is going to make up for the interest that is going to build up on any balance that you have on those cards. Your best bet is to just stay away from the credit cards.

Student loan debt is also an area where we would want to have no debt. I made the mistake, myself, of running up large student loans for my MBA from Emory. It is something I wish I had not done.

There are other avenues of education that do not require huge student loans. A couple of ways to keep education costs down are to go to inexpensive state schools for undergraduate degree programs and to consider professional designations, rather than expensive graduate-degree programs.

It has been my experience that professional designations carry much more weight in most professions than do graduate degrees. For instance, even though I have the two graduate degrees, every person I have interviewed, regarding the finance industry has asked if I had completed or was planning to complete the Chartered Financial Analyst program. The same holds true for the Professional Engineer, Certified Financial Planner, Project Manager Certification, and so on.

There are a few professions where an advanced degree is preferred and often required. A couple of these areas are the medical field and the field of law. You must go to medical school or law school, if you want to practice in one of these fields. In these cases, you must carefully weigh all of the future benefits against all of the costs of obtaining these degrees. Some hidden costs that are often not considered are the interest on the loans for school, the lost opportunity for wages while in school, the lost opportunity to invest the money elsewhere that will go to loans, and the possibility of not getting a high-paying job in the field, once the degree program is complete. All of these issues should be weighed carefully before making such a large financial decision. I did not do a good job of analyzing these costs, when I made the decision to go to school at Emory, and I wish that I had.

Structuring and Eliminating Debt

The main culprit that keeps us from realizing our financial dreams and having the freedom we want in our lives is debt. Let's face it, the main reason we go to work every morning is probably because we owe someone money. Otherwise, we could save up enough to pay our monthly bills and take some time off from work. So, if we want to ever have a chance of not being forced to go to work every day, the first thing we need to do is to get rid of debt.

So, how do we do that? What is a practical plan that allows us to pay down our debts in the shortest amount of time? Well, we are going to try to answer that here.

The first thing we want to do is look at the type of debts we have, then the amounts. A lot of people will say that you should pay off the smallest debt first and then move on to the next debt by using all of the money you were paying on the first debt to pay down the second one more quickly. I believe this is partially true. I do believe, however, that there are a couple of flaws with this thinking.

The first flaw I see is that the interest rate on each of the different debts you have is not taken into consideration. If you have a loan for $1000 at an interest rate of 6 percent per year and a credit card debt of $5000 at an interest rate of 29.9 percent per year, which one do you want to pay down first? Which one is costing you more money in interest each year? This principle is very similar to our example, above, of looking at all of the costs of a college education loan instead of just the loan amount

Now, there are some caveats to this way of thinking. If you can pay off one of the loans in one year and the other debt is going to take you five years, then by all means pay off the quicker one first. I am just saying that it is not always as simple as paying off the smallest debt first.

The other flaw I see is that you should take part of the freed up money that you now have each month from paying off the first debt and put it into savings, or put it into an investment fund that will generate money for you down the road. This has a couple of benefits. The first one is that you can see yourself actually accumulating money, as well as paying off debt. The second benefit is that you are generating more money with which to pay down debt, later.

A rule I follow is that I take half the money I have available each month for extra debt payments and split that between my savings and my investment account. This allows me to save money for a rainy day, invest for my future, and still pay down my debts.

You may not like doing it that way. Debt may be a very stressful thing for you, and your goal may be to get out of it as quickly as possible. That is fine, too. Just take into consideration the things I noted, above. Decide which debt you are going to pay off first by looking at, not only how quickly you can pay the debt off, but also by how much interest you are paying each year on that debt.

Determining Which Items Can Be Borrowed For

This section is very important to your financial health over the long term. There are several different categories of things that can be borrowed for. Some of these categories include feel-good items, education, transportation, and housing. These are the major categories. Of course, there are more, but these are the major ones that we will focus on.

So what types of items are covered by these categories? Housing is pretty self-explanatory. This is the house you will live in the majority of the time—your permanent residence. Transportation is also fairly self-explanatory. Transportation refers to the vehicle you will use most of the time to get yourself to and from work and to run your daily errands. Education can cover several different things, such as your own college or graduate education, your child's private school or college education, a professional certification, or a seminar that you feel like will make you a more successful person in some way.

The last category contains the things that I refer to as feel-good items. These include anything that is bought on a whim, a second home, an automobile purchased for enjoyment only, a boat, or any other big-kid toy. These also include the vast majority of items purchased on a credit card. Credit card purchases usually include clothes, vacations, nights out on the town, or many other various items not essential to our lives.

Now, which type of debt do we want to talk about first? Let's start with feel-good items. Feel-good items are the main culprits that ruin our financial lives. These are the things that we need to feel fulfilled or to keep up with the neighbors down the street. These are the things that we can do without. If we can do without them, then why would we ever want to go into debt to have them? We wouldn't! Now, I am not going to tell you that you can never purchase feel-good items, but you should purchase them only after you have saved up for them and can purchase them with cash. We will talk about how to save up for them in our savings section coming up shortly.

Education is the next item on the list. We have already talked quite a bit about education in the first chapter, so I won't bore you with another rehashing of the information. Just remember to look at all of the factors that go into paying for an education, to determine if it will be worth it in the end. You should always look at education as an investment. Then the key question becomes: Am I going to get a good return on my time and money invested? Remember to look at these factors:

- Cheaper alternatives
- Professional designations
- Interest paid on loans, as well as the loan amount
- Time spent on the education that could be spent elsewhere
- Money lost by being a student instead of working
- The possibility of not getting the high-paying job for which you are going to school

After all of these things are considered, then and only then, should you proceed with the decision to pursue the education.

Transportation is the next item we will consider. With the exception of a house and possibly your education (if you don't consider the things I have laid out above), a car is probably going to be the largest purchase you will make. With that in mind, this is a decision you must make very carefully. Like the education decision, there are many factors that should be looked at when deciding which car to purchase.

There are many hidden costs that come with car ownership that most people do not consider when determining which car to purchase. These costs include the interest on the loan, auto tag registration taxes each year, regular maintenance costs, gasoline costs, and insurance costs. All of these costs take a chunk out of your monthly paycheck.

With this in mind, the ideal car purchase is one where you do not have to take out a loan. Paying cash for a car that you can afford is the easiest on your wallet. By not having to pay a car payment each month, you can focus on your other debts and your savings.

Of course, owning a nice car is mostly about vanity. It says to the world that you have made it and that you have good taste. A car says something about who you are. Because of this, I know that most people would rather go into debt to drive a nicer car, than pay cash for a less expensive car. Because of this, I have developed a rule to allow you to buy a little more car. The rule is this: you must put at least 50 percent down on the car you purchase and you should not finance it for more than three years. This rule ensures that you will not buy more car than you can afford and that your payment will be manageable each month.

The last thing we want to do is to get in trouble with our monthly expenses or not be able to put money into savings or investments because we bought too much car. After all, a car is really just a machine that transports us from point A to point B.

Finally, we have the home purchase. If you are not going to live in a place for more than five years, you should rent. Do not lock yourself into a location because you bought a house and cannot get rid of it. Many of the rules in this book come from mistakes I have made. I have made this one, too.

We have been led to believe that everyone should own a huge house—the bigger the better. We have been told that the size of our house and the neighborhood where we live says something about who we are. Do you know who has been feeding us this garbage? The bankers and the homebuilders—they are the ones getting rich, while we are the ones stuck working the rest of our lives to pay for a house that is too big for our income.

The rule for determining how much house we can reasonably afford is this: put 20 percent down and finance the house over fifteen years. This is a fixed fifteen-year mortgage, not some bank creation where you pay interest only for a portion of the time. Ideally, you will be able to pay the house off in less than fifteen years, when you have paid off all of your other debts.

If you cannot put 20 percent down on a house or afford to finance it for fifteen years or less, then you need to keep looking for a house that fits those criteria. With today's housing market being what it is, foreclosures and short sales are everywhere. If you cannot find a fully-priced house that meets your financial and personal criteria, then look in the foreclosure and short-sale market. Auctions are held nearly every month in most areas of the country.

A great resource for getting an idea of the short sales, foreclosures, and auction homes in your area is Auction.com. I get their monthly flier, which lists all of the homes coming up for auction in my area over the next month. You may even be able to find a home you like and strike a deal with the owner before it goes to auction.

Establishing a Savings Plan

Your savings account is a very important piece of your financial picture. This is where you will have your emergency funds, your money for big-ticket items you want to purchase, and your fun money. Some people advise having separate accounts for all of these things, but I think that is confusing.

The first thing that you will want to establish in your savings account is a six-month emergency fund. This emergency fund will be the mount of money you would need to pay your bills for six months, if you were to lose your job. This does not include the amount of money you put towards investments and savings each month, just the money you will need to pay your bills and buy groceries—basically the money that it will take for you to continue living at your current level, until you can find another job.

Once you have accumulated the six-month emergency fund, then you can start adding to the fund for items that you are saving up to buy, like a new car, a vacation, a shopping trip for fun, or any other thing that you might want to spend money on in the future. This is also where you will accumulate the money for the 20 percent down payment on a house or the 50 percent down payment or full purchase of a new car.

Your feel-good money will come from this fund as well. This money is added to the fund over and above the emergency funds and the big-ticket item funds.

As you see this fund grow, while your debts shrink, you will have the double satisfaction of knowing that you are building your wealth, while shrinking what you owe. Ultimately, we want to be working only on growing our wealth and have nothing that we owe.

Establishing An Investment/Cash-Generation Plan

Along with building your savings account, you should be building your investment account. This will be money that you will use for retirement or any other need that may arise in the future. This is the account that is going to eventually provide your financial freedom.

You should fund this account in equal proportion to your savings account. That is, for every dollar that you put in your savings account, you should put a dollar into your investment account. In my view, this is probably the most important piece of your financial picture. Yet, most people know the least about this part of the financial equation. That is why the rest of this book will be focused on investing. I will explain investing to you in simple terms, the way it should be taught to everyone. After all, investing is not very difficult; Wall Street, however, just wants you to think that it is difficult, so that they can take your money from you.

There are a lot of different assets you can invest in to grow your money and produce income. We will focus on investing in stocks, bonds, and commodities in this book. Some other investments include income-producing real estate, owner-absentee small businesses, and private-business investment. These are all good options, if you are willing to invest the time to learn about and be involved with them, but we will focus on investments that will take as little of your time as possible, while still generating nice returns over the long term.

Enjoying Your Money

The last part of the financial picture is enjoying your money. After all, we all work to have nice things and to enjoy life. Your money should definitely bring you enjoyment, but you have to decide whether you want to enjoy your money, now, and go into debt, or save your money and enjoy it later.

Obviously, I recommend becoming debt free, saving your money, and enjoying it later. That is not to say that you cannot enjoy any of it now. Of course you can. That is why we established the feel-good portion of the savings account. Just make sure that you keep the enjoyment of your money limited to the amount that you put away for the feel-good items. In the long term, being disciplined this way and not having to worry about debt will make you much happier.

Chapter Summary

One thing I have not mentioned until now is that there are tools on the Internet that help you establish and track your budget each month. These tools will allow you to enter and track your income, bills, debt, savings, and investment account. This is a really nice way to view everything in one place, rather than trying to pull it all together yourself. My favorite tool to use is Mint.com.

I know we covered a lot of material in this chapter, so I have laid it all out using the bullet points below. Refer back to this list whenever you need a checkup on your personal finance strategy.

Main points from this chapter:

- Set up a monthly budget.
- Spend a maximum 35 percent of monthly income for housing.
- Spend a maximum 15 percent of monthly income for a car payment.
- Use coupons and rewards cards for groceries.
- Shop rates for power, telephone, cable/ Internet, and insurance once per year.
- Reduce cable/Internet costs by eliminating extras, such as premium channels and DVR.
- Eliminate cable altogether and use Internet sites, such as fancast.com and hulu.com for television viewing.
- Never buy a new car just to reduce gas costs.
- Never use credit cards; they are financial suicide.

- Consider alternatives to education, which requires student loans.
- Carefully weigh hidden costs when considering student loans.
- Evaluate interest rates, as well as time to pay off each debt, when choosing which debt to attack first.
- As you pay off debt, split the newly freed-up money equally between savings/investments and paying off debt.
- Never borrow for feel-good items—save up for those items.
- Consider all hidden costs associated with car ownership, when making an auto purchase.
- Make the auto purchase goal to pay for the car in full with cash.
- Pay 50 percent, as a down payment and finance for no more than three years, if you must take out a loan for a car.
- Rent instead, if you are not going to live in a place for more than five years.
- Pay 20 percent as a down payment and finance for no more than fifteen years, using a fixed mortgage, when you purchase a home.
- Look at short sales and foreclosures, always, when looking to buy a home—auction.com is one source.
- Establish a savings account for a six-month emergency fund, big ticket items, and fun money.

- Fund your investment account in equal proportion to your savings account.
- Enjoy your fun money by purchasing feel-good items; personal finance should be fun, so enjoy some of your hard earned money.
- Use Internet tools to track all of your finances in one place—mint.com is one source.

Chapter 3

~ ECONOMICS ~

As difficult as the world's economists try to make this subject, it is actually a pretty simple subject. Economics is essentially the study of the flow of capital. In other words, money flows around the world and accumulates in the places where it is treated best.

You can think of money (capital) like water. As water moves towards the ocean, it moves through the places where it meets the least resistance. It fills up low-lying areas to create ponds, lakes, and rivers.

This is the same with money. It flows to the places where it is treated best. Unlike the amount of water in the world, however, the amount of capital in the world is not fixed.

The amount of money in the world used to be relatively fixed, because it was backed by gold or silver in some form. There have been times throughout history when money was not backed by gold or silver, and those forms of money always ended in disaster for the people who used it.

The dollar became the currency used by the rest of the world to conduct trade. This is what is meant when the dollar is referred to as the world's reserve currency. So, countries all over the world had to accumulate dollars to conduct international trade. In this sense, the dollar was really the first world currency.

The dollar was chosen because it was still backed by gold after World War II. Also, the United States accumulated the majority of the world's gold during the war, as other countries purchased our weapons and supplies.

Because the dollar was backed by gold, it could be redeemed for gold. So the countries that held dollars could come to the United States government and ask to exchange their paper dollars for gold. This worked for a while, until other countries decided that they too should redeem their dollars for gold, before the United States ran out.

The problem we faced was that we had printed too many dollars and did not have enough gold to give, in exchange for the dollars that were being redeemed.

Another huge problem we faced was that, like most Western Countries, we had a central bank printing our money for us. We outsourced the printing of our money to a private bank in 1913. That bank is known as the Federal Reserve. It has private shareholders, just like any other bank. The problem is that these shareholders are never revealed, because the bank is private, and its stock is not traded publicly. Suffice it to say that the richest people, corporations, and nations own shares in the Federal Reserve Bank.

Why is it a problem to have a private bank print our money? Well, it presents several problems, the biggest of which is that we have to create debt, in order to get dollars. If our government wants to get dollars to spend, we have to create treasury bonds to get those dollars. Basically, a treasury bond is a loan from the Federal Reserve.

So, how does this fit into our gold-backing situation? Well, since it was possible after 1913 to just create debt to get dollars, the US government lost control of their budget, and they began to run up larger and larger needs for dollars. Because we only had a fixed amount of gold, we had to print more dollars using debt than we could by mining and accumulating gold.

This takes us back to the problem we faced when the countries tried to redeem their dollars for gold. We had flooded the world with dollars, and we did not have the gold to exchange for them. As a result, in 1971, President Nixon officially removed the gold backing from the dollar. This was technically a default on the United States Monetary system.

Since 1971, we have had no real backing to the dollar. Neither has any other country on Earth. So we have been running an experiment where countries print as much debt as they want and sell that debt to other countries and their own central banks in exchange for money. The US has even been selling these bonds to its own citizens for decades.

So, why am I telling you all of this? It is important that you know how money is created, in order to understand how it flows around the world. It is also important for you to understand that the debt these countries are creating will never be repaid. There is no possible way that the United States can pay back $14.25 trillion dollars. The total amount of value that the US economy produces each year (Gross Domestic Product—GDP) is currently at $14.7 trillion.

Study after study suggests that economies of countries that reach 90 percent debt to GDP begin to weaken, and the government spending in those countries spirals out of control, as they have to pay more and more interest on that debt. There is only one thing you can do in that situation—declare bankruptcy.

According to a recent article from the National Inflation Association[1], the US budget deficit for 2011 is projected to be $1.645 trillion, which is 43 percent of the total 2011 budget of $3.819 trillion. On a percentage basis, this is very close to Brazil's budget deficit in 1993 and Bolivia's budget deficit in 1985, right before those two economies began to experience hyperinflation.

According to NIA, the only way that a country with percentage budget deficits that high can continue on without experiencing hyperinflation is if foreign countries continue lending to the country with the high-budget deficits. This presents a problem, because the same article notes that the private sector of the US has completely stopped purchasing US government debt; foreign countries have reduced their purchases from 50 percent of all purchases to 30 percent. The Federal Reserve has stepped in to take up the slack. They have recently increased their purchases from 10 percent of US Treasury Bonds sold to 70 percent. When our own central bank is purchasing the bulk of our debt, we are in for serious trouble ahead.

We are not at the default/hyperinflation point just yet, but we are getting very close. So what happens between now and then? We are supposed to be talking about economics, right? How is the money flowing around the world today, and how is it likely to flow in the future?

Well, as I said above, money flows where it is treated best. That is to say that money will flow to the places where it is rewarded without much risk. For the last thirty years, that place has been in the United States, specifically in US Treasury Bonds. Some of the reasons for this are these:

- The dollar is the world's reserve currency.
- The United States used to encourage capitalism and innovation so, therefore, we became the world's largest economy.
- The United States has never officially defaulted on its debt before.
- The United States is the strongest country in the world, militarily.
- Wall Street has been the engine that directed money flow around the world for the last several decades.

Because of these things, our economy was viewed as very stable, and investors knew that they would be able to obtain some interest on their money without the risk of losing it to a government debt default.

In the past year or two, we have started to see money flow into other areas, such as commodities and stocks. This is because people are starting to realize that the governments of the United States and the European countries that have been using debt as a way to finance all of their unsustainable social programs will never be able to repay those debts. So, now, the risk of losing the money is greater than the reward of interest paid on the money.

We are likely to see this trend gain strength over the next few years. Governments will find it more and more difficult to find purchasers of their debts, while the citizens of those countries will become increasingly angry with those governments for taking away their social benefits.

So, where will the money flow, and what will happen when it flows there? Well, there is one more thing we need to address to fully understand how money flows and to find where it is treated best. We have already discussed the flooding of the world with money backed by nothing. Now, we need to discuss how governments attract or repel money through taxes and tariffs.

Along with the Federal Reserve act in 1913, which established the Federal Reserve Bank as the United States central bank, was the enactment of the Revenue Act. The Revenue Act imposed federal income taxes on the citizens of the United States. This is always the first step in reducing the economic prosperity of a country. As taxes on individuals and companies increase, those individuals and companies will move to countries where they will pay lower taxes. For instance, the current corporate tax rate in the US is 35 percent, whereas in Ireland it is currently 12.5 percent. Corporations are moving from the US to Ireland at an alarming rate. These companies can't seem to get there fast enough.

Labor and innovation always want to be rewarded. Otherwise, there is no reason for labor and innovation to exist. The more you reduce the reward, the more you discourage labor and innovation. Since money is just the physical representative of the reward for labor and innovation, the more of it a government takes away, the more that government discourages labor and innovation within its borders. In other words, the higher a government raises its taxes, the more it will encourage labor and innovation to move to another, more friendly country.

So, if the US and Europe are making things difficult for labor and innovation, what countries are rewarding labor and innovation? Currently, two of the biggest countries rewarding innovation and labor are China and Brazil. These two countries are growing rapidly and are providing very attractive opportunities for money to thrive. These two countries will continue to see money flow into their borders, as long as they continue to provide safe, attractive environments for the labor and innovation that are located there.

A few other countries that will attract money, as the western countries fall from economic dominance, will be Panama, Costa Rica, Chile, and Hong Kong, as well as a few others. These countries are currently providing favorable tax incentives for people and businesses. Will these tax incentives last? We can't be sure. Governments always get greedy at some point or another, but for now, they are worth a look.

The next question becomes, will all of the money flow to China and Brazil? No it won't. There will still be opportunity in the US and Europe. It will just be harder to keep the money that is made within the borders of these countries. As the world is flooded with Euros and Dollars, prices will continue to rise. Also, as these governments go into more and more debt, they will continue to try to grab all of the money they can from their citizens.

Let's say we are willing to take the chance and keep our money in these countries. What should we invest in? Well, the best investments are going to be solid, undervalued companies, precious metals, and commodities. As I have described above, as it becomes more and more obvious that governments will never repay their debts, the money that is currently invested and which will be invested in these debts will flow into real, tangible assets. The three main areas that should receive the bulk of the money are stocks, precious metals, and commodities. These are my favorite investments for the foreseeable future.

Main points from this chapter:

- Economics is the study of the flow of capital.
- Money (capital) flows to the places it is treated best.
- Money flows like water.
- The United States dollar was backed by gold until 1971.
- The US dollar has been the world's reserve currency since World War II.
- Money flowed into government debt for the last thirty years.
- The United States and European governments are going further and further into debt.
- These governments will likely never be able to repay those debts.
- As these governments get more and more desperate, they increase taxes on citizens and businesses.
- This causes wealthy citizens and businesses to flee to other countries.
- China, Brazil, Panama, Costa Rica, Chile, and Hong Kong are currently attracting a lot of money.

- Money is beginning to flow away from government debt.
- Money will most likely flow into stocks, precious metals, and commodities in the coming years.

Chapter 4

~VALUING BUSINESSES ~

Most of the financial media and brokers on Wall Street want you to believe that stocks are pieces of paper that are to be traded, as their prices go up and down. They want you to believe that the price of the stock is the only thing that matters. This could not be further from the truth.

You see, they want you to be short-term traders, so that they can continue to rack up brokerage fees. If they can constantly assault you with all of the minute-to-minute changes taking place in the markets, then they can convince you that the stocks that you hold need to be sold and other stocks need to be bought. This is not investing. This is speculating. We will cover speculating in more depth, later, but for now just understand that very few people make long-term money by speculating.

Investing, on the other hand, requires a completely different approach. It requires that you view the investments that you are making as long-term investments. If you were going to purchase a small business in your hometown, you would not buy that business and then sell it three weeks later. You would do the research it took to completely understand that business, and then you would buy it with the intent that it would make you money over the long term.

The world's best investor—Warren Buffett—takes exactly this approach. He makes investments based on the benefit that the investment is likely to provide him over time. The world's best investors typically take this approach.

As a matter of fact, whenever you start to see the majority people taking short-term approaches to a an area of investment (real estate, stocks, commodities, precious metals, etc.), you can be sure that the best investors have reduced their holdings in that area and a collapse is coming. That is the difference between the average investor and the world's greatest investors.

So, why am I telling you this? It is important for you to understand that the typical approach that average investors take is exactly the wrong approach. You also need to understand that the vast majority of the financial world is going to tell you that you should be making decisions about your investments on a very short-term basis. They want you to believe that the daily market price of your investment is what the investment is worth.

It takes a lot of confidence, guts, discipline, and determination to stick with an investment, whose price may have dropped 50 percent from when you bought it.

These are exactly the characteristics you need to have, however, to invest for the long term. It is essential that you not get caught up in the day-to-day price movements of your investments, if you want to be successful over time. It has even been said that Warren Buffett does not even have a computer on his desk, and that he cannot tell you what any of his investments are trading at on any given day.

So, how does he have this confidence, and how can we get it, too? He has this confidence in his investments because he knows the true value of his investments. He knows what his companies are worth, and he knows that he has purchased them at prices that are well below their true value.

In other words, it is kind of like going to the grocery store and finding your favorite food items are on sale for 25 percent of what they usually sell for. If you get home and find that you had a coupon that would have saved you another 10 percent, would you be upset? Would you want to go back to the store and get a refund for the item? I would certainly hope not. You would probably be pretty happy that you were able to get such a great deal in the first place.

This should be your approach when it comes to investments, as well. When you see an investment that is selling for much less than what it is worth, you should want to purchase as much of that investment as you can afford. You won't put all of your money into it, but you will put in the amount that you have predetermined that you can invest into any one investment. We will cover how to make this determination later.

So, how do we know if an investment is undervalued? Is the process different for stocks, commodities, precious metals, and other investments? The simple answer is yes, the process is different for each of them, but the overall approach is the same. You want to buy things for much less than they are worth.

So, how do we determine how much something is worth? In this chapter, we will learn how to value businesses, so that you will know which stocks to invest in. In later chapters, we will discuss precious metals and commodities. By the end of the book, you will hopefully have a road map and a solid understanding of how to approach investment to determine exactly what to purchase, and in what amounts, according to the total amount of investment money that you have.

Valuing businesses does not have to be as difficult as you might imagine. As a matter of fact, Wall Street seems to throw all kinds of crazy numbers out, so that it seems very confusing. If you were to value a small business that you were going to purchase, you would really only need know a few things:

- How much does the business sell annually?
- What business is the company involved in?
- Have the sales been growing or shrinking over the last few years?
- How much are your annual operating costs?
- How much debt does the company have?
- How much cash does the company have?
- What kind of earnings does the company generate?

These are really the basic things you need to know, when you are valuing a company. The last question that should come up is, "How much are they asking for the company?" This is because you want to have a good idea of what the company does and how much it is actually worth, before you start to worry about the price you will need to pay.

So, how do we find the answers to these questions? Is it difficult to find the answers to these questions? It is actually much easier than you have been led to believe. You do not need to have a degree in finance to determine what a company is worth and whether it is currently selling for less than it is worth. A few key figures will tell you what you need to know.

Now, the accountants and financial analysts are going to freak out when I give you these figures and tell you that these figures are all you need to know. They make a living making things complicated and digging through details. That is great for them, but we are not attempting to be analysts or accountants; we are investors.

A famous Warren Buffett rule is that a company should be able to be valued with a few simple calculations on the back of a napkin. If that is good enough for him, it should be good enough for us. As a matter of fact, you would be very surprised at the number of multi-billion-dollar deals that are done with just a few simple calculations to determine the value of the asset being purchased.

So, what are these key figures to look for? They are actually ratios. They are Price/Intrinsic Value and Enterprise Value/EBITDA. I know. I know. Those look complicated, and you probably think you will never be able to figure them out. Don't worry. We are going to walk through every step (which are just a few).

Let's start with intrinsic value—what is it? Intrinsic value is the true value of the company. It is not the price at which the company may be currently selling. An example is a car that is valued at $18,000, based on popular automobile valuing websites. Let's say the seller of the car really needs the cash from selling the car, so he is willing to sell the car for $14,000. Is the car now worth $14,000? No, it is still worth $18,000, but the buyer was able to get a good deal on the car. This is an example of how intrinsic value—the real value—of a company can differ form the price at which it is selling.

So, how do we determine intrinsic value? There are several ways to calculate intrinsic value. My favorite way to calculate intrinsic value is by using a formula that is often referred to as the Benjamin Graham Formula. Benjamin Graham, who was Warren Buffett's teacher, devised this formula. He wrote about this formula in his famous book, *Security Analysis*, which he published back in 1962. The formula is as follows:

V= EPS x (8.5 +2g)
Where:
V= Intrinsic Value
EPS = Earnings Per Share

8.5 = Price/Earnings Ratio for a no growth company

g = expected growth rate of the company over the next seven to ten years

An alternative version of the formula, which features later Graham revisions, is as follows:

$$V = \frac{EPSx(8.5 + 2g)x4.4}{Y}$$

Where:

V= Intrinsic Value

EPS = Earnings Per Share

8.5 = Price/Earnings Ratio for a no growth company

g = expected growth rate of the company over the next seven to ten years

4.4 = Average yield (interest rate) on AAA rated corporate bonds in 1962

Y = The current yield (interest rate) on AAA corporate rated bonds

Don't worry about finding all of these values and learning how to use the formula. There are plenty of intrinsic value calculators and screeners online. One of my favorites is a screener at www. grahaminvestor.com. There are several others, if you just run a Google search using the term "intrinsic value calculator."

So, what do we do, once we have calculated our estimated intrinsic value? We simply divide the current price of one share of the company's stock by the estimated intrinsic value. This will give us a percentage. You can view this as the percentage that you will have to pay of the company's true value. The lower the percentage the better. I prefer not to pay more than 25 percent of intrinsic value, but many people believe that paying up to 66 percent of intrinsic value still allows room for good returns. They are correct, but my belief is that we should try to get the best deal we can for our money.

So, now that we have the intrinsic value formula figured out, let's see which of our questions above the formula answers. It answers the following questions:

- How much does the business sell annually?
- Have the sales been growing or shrinking over the last few years?
- What kind of earnings does the company generate?

So, what do we need to use to answer the remaining questions? For those answers, we will look at Enterprise Value/EBITDA.

What is "Enterprise Value?" Enterprise Value is the value of all of the company's stock at the current price, plus all of the company's debt, minus all of the company's cash. This figure basically tells us what we will have to pay to purchase the whole company, along with all of its debt, after we use the existing cash to pay debt. It sounds complicated, but it is really not. Luckily, this value is easily found for each company, with a little searching on most financial sites such as Yahoo! Finance.

Now, what is EBITDA? EBITDA is essentially the earnings of the company before it pays an interest on its debt and taxes. The acronym EBITDA actually stands for "earnings before interest, taxes, depreciation, and amortization." Why would we want to know the EBITDA? Well, a lot of companies use different accounting tricks to try to inflate their earnings numbers. EBITDA lets us compare companies before their accountants can use those tricks.

EBITDA is basically the value of all of the company's sales for the year, minus all of the company's costs of doing business. This is the amount of money you would likely be left with, before you paid your taxes, if you were a small business owner.

So, why are Enterprise Value and EBITDA important? These numbers answer the following questions:

- How much are your annual operating costs?
- How much debt does the company have?
- How much cash does the company have?

These answers tell us what the company looks like from a debt perspective and whether the current share price is cheap, based on the assets and debt of the company. This ratio—EV/EBITDA—is actually one of the key metrics that private equity firms use, when they decide how much to pay for a company that they potentially want to purchase. It is also used when companies want to purchase other companies.

If it is used so often, how do we know if we are using it correctly? How do we know when this ratio is telling us if we are getting a good deal or not? We will want to know if this company is a good candidate for a potential buyout, based on this ratio. If it is good enough for a private equity firm or a competitor to buy it, it is good enough for us.

So, what is a good number to use for this ratio? What number are firms using to determine their offer prices for firms, today? Gymboree was recently sold for 7.7 x EV/EBITDA and Family Dollar was recently offered 10 x EV/EBITDA to buy out their company. Based on these and many other deals in recent history, we will use 10 EV/EBITDA as our ceiling for determining if a company is undervalued.

Now we have determined how to value a company. We have answered all of the basic questions except one: What business is the company involved in? There is no formula for that question. You will have to do a little Internet researching to find out the answer to that. A simple Google search or visit to the company's website should provide you with the answer to that question. Now that we know how to value a company, we will learn how to use this knowledge to pick undervalued stocks in the next chapter.

Main points from this chapter:

- Investing requires a long-term view.
- Investing requires confidence, guts, discipline, and determination.
- Investing requires that you view your stock purchases, as you would buying a small business in your hometown.
- Valuing businesses requires you to answer seven vital questions, which are listed below:
  1. How much does the business sell annually?
  2. What business is the company involved in?
  3. Have the sales been growing or shrinking over the last few years?
  4. How much are the annual operating costs?
  5. How much debt does the company have?
  6. How much cash does the company have?
  7. What kind of earnings does the company generate?

- To answer these questions, we use the Price/Intrinsic Value and Enterprise Value/EBITDA ratios.
- Price/Intrinsic Value answers our questions about earnings and growth.
- Enterprise Value/EBITDA answers our questions about operating costs, cash, and debt.
- Enterprise Value/EBITDA gives us a picture of whether a company is cheap enough for a potential buyout by a competitor or investment firm.

Chapter 5

~ SELECTING STOCKS ~

Now that we have learned how to value companies, we will learn how to apply that knowledge and information to picking stocks to invest in. We will use both of our ratios to pick these stocks. We will apply both ratios in a specific way to find the ones that are the most undervalued. Again, this may seem difficult, but with a little practice, it will become second nature to you.

To recap, we will use 25 percent Price/Intrinsic Value and 10 EV/EBITDA as our cutoffs to determine if a company is undervalued or not. How do we combine these values to determine exactly which companies are undervalued and are selling at a level we can feel comfortable investing in? I have come up with a formula that takes both values into account. It allows us to put them both into percentage form and add them to come up with a total percentage. It is what I refer to as my Percent of Value Formula.

The formula is as follows:

$$\%V = \frac{Price}{Intrinsic\,Value} + \frac{EV\,/\,EBITDA}{10}$$

Here is an example:

If stock is currently selling at $15.00 and we calculate the intrinsic value at $75.00 then the Price/Intrinsic Value = 15/75 = 20%. Then we look at the EV/EBITDA ratio, which can be found in the key statistics section for each stock at Yahoo! Finance. Let's say that ratio is 5. We will divide 5 by 10 to get 50%. We will then add 50% to 20% in order to get a total percent of value (%V) of 70%.

We will do this for all of the stocks we are looking to invest in. Then we will rank them all from lowest %V to highest %V. We will then purchase the stocks with the lowest %V. This allows us to find the most undervalued stocks from our list.

So, how many stocks should we buy? What should we expect from the stocks that we buy? How long should we hold these stocks? Should we ever buy more of any of the stocks that we already own? These are some of the questions we will answer throughout the rest of this chapter.

So, how many stocks should we buy? The short answer is—it depends. It depends on how much money we have to invest. Because we never want to put more than 60 percent of our portfolio into value stocks, the number of stocks we are going to hold will depend on the overall amount of money we have to invest. I will lay out the exact makeup of the model portfolio later in the book.

Because the typical online brokerage account charges somewhere between $7 and $10 per trade, we will want to invest at least $500 in each stock. A $10 commission on a $500 purchase is 2 percent that we have to make up with our investment, before we even get started. Throw in another $10, when and if we sell the stock down the road, and that is 4 percent of the original stock purchase in fees alone. This is why we never want to put less than $500 in any one stock.

Let's say you have $10,000 to invest, and 60 percent of that goes into value stocks. That means you have $6000 to invest in value stocks. This means that you can buy 12 value stocks, if you put $500 into each one. This is a pretty good number to give you diversification, but also keep your portfolio small enough that you can still keep up with each company. I would say that fifteen stocks is probably the upper limit to hold at any one time, unless you are dealing with very large sums of money.

What should you expect from the stocks you buy? Because you are buying stocks that are undervalued, you should not expect them to increase in price right away. Stocks that are undervalued are typically hated by the market for one reason or another. They may be in an industry that is not popular at the moment, or they may just be overlooked. Whatever the case, don't expect the market to suddenly change its view on them, as soon as you buy the stock.

In fact, the stock price may continue to go down for a while after you make your purchase. As long as the company is performing well in its operations and continues to make money, don't worry about the stock price fluctuations. Over the long term, you can expect the stock price to move back towards the company's intrinsic value. This is where you will make your money. It may take a while, and it may be scary along the way, but as long as the company continues to perform well, you will eventually make money.

How long should you expect to hold these stocks? Again, the answer is, it depends. Benjamin Graham advocated holding the stock for at least two years, to give it time to move back towards its true value. Warren Buffett says that you should never buy a stock that you will not be comfortable holding forever. This goes back to viewing the investment as a purchase of ownership in the company and its operation, not a purchase of a stock that fluctuates in price.

My view falls somewhere in between these two. We should be prepared to hold the stock of any company that we invest in for at least two years, and maybe more, if the stock price has not yet moved up to acceptable levels. We will typically only sell a stock when one of three things happens:

1. The stock rises to at least 80 percent of its intrinsic value.
2. The %V rises to 1.7 or more.
3. The company gets bought out and its stock is retired.
4. Something happens with the company that changes our view of it, such as a sustained downturn in sales, accounting scandals, or anything else that negatively affects the operations of the company's business going forward.

These are the three things to watch for when determining when to sell the stock of a company you have invested in. Remember that you must always view yourself as a partial owner of the business, and you should always act as you would if you were a majority owner of the business. How would you view your ownership of that business if you were the majority owner? What decisions would you make regarding when to sell your stake in the company?

Should we ever invest more money into a company after we have made our initial investment? The short answer is yes, under certain conditions. As we continue to add to our investment account—we are doing that every month along with our savings, right?—We will have more and more money in our account that needs to be invested. After we have fully invested our portfolio in the proper proportions of stocks and commodities, and we hold the maximum number of investments that we are comfortable with, then we should begin investing more into investments that we already hold.

How do we know which investments to add money to? We want to add to investments that we consider to still be undervalued at the time of investment. If you really like a company that has moved up in price, but which is still below 50 percent of its intrinsic value, then it would probably be acceptable to add money to your initial investment. The ideal situation, however, would be to add money to a stock that has dropped in price, but one in which the company is continuing to perform to our expectations. This allows you to pick up more of the investment at an even lower price, which lowers the total price paid for the investment.

We have covered a lot about investing in determining the value of and investing in the stock of companies in the last two chapters. There has been a lot of technical information to absorb. If you need to take some time to let the information soak in, or go back and read through the information, go ahead and do that now. From here, we are going to move on to other areas of investment, particularly commodities, silver and gold, bonds, and speculation—in that order.

Main points from this chapter:

- We us the Percent of Value Formula to determine which stocks are the most undervalued:

$$\%V = \frac{Price}{Intrinsic\,Value} + \frac{EV\,/\,EBITDA}{10}$$

- We then rank the stocks in order from lowest %V to highest %V and begin buying the stocks with the lowest %V.
- We buy a maximum of fifteen stocks, based on how much money we have to invest.
- We should never expect the stocks that we purchase to immediately start increasing in price. The market is overlooking them for some reason. They may even continue to move down in price for a while.
- We never invest less than $500 into a stock because of the cost of fees.
- Never invest more than 60 percent of your investment money into value stocks.
- We always hold a stock at least two years, unless the price has reached 80 percent of intrinsic value or more, the %V is 1.7 or

more, the company is bought out and the stock is retired, or the performance of the business has changed in some negative way.

- We can invest more money into a stock only after we have invested in a fifteen value stocks and invested the other 40 percent of our money into the other assets that we will cover in the following chapters.

- Ideally, we want to add money to stocks that have moved down in price, but a company that is still performing as we expected.

Chapter 6

~ COMMODITIES ~

What are commodities, and why should we care about them? Why are they an asset we should be concerned with? What makes them so valuable? Why are they not talked about more in the media? Why is there so little reference to them in the financial world? We will answer these questions and more in this chapter in our effort to help you understand commodities and their very large place in our lives.

Commodities are the basic materials that we consume, either directly or indirectly, in our daily lives. These are the materials that are used to make our food, shelter, energy, clothing, and consumer products. They are things like wood, oil, meat, copper, steel, cotton, corn, wheat, soybeans, and on an on. They are the things that grow in our fields, are pulled from the earth, and cut down for our use. Without them, we could not survive, and we certainly would not be able to thrive as we do today.

Many people throughout history have attempted to control the production of a few of these commodities. During the times they were able to control them, those people became extremely wealthy. A couple of examples are Andrew Carnegie with steel and John D. Rockefeller with oil. They saw the need for these materials in modern, industrial nations, and they made fortunes by attempting to become the major supplier of these materials.

Now are we going to be able to control the vast supply of these materials? No, but we can invest in these materials on a much smaller scale. If we cannot control the production of these materials, then why should we invest in them? Will we still make money, even if we can't control their supply? Yes. Just like value stocks, over a long period of time we can make money investing in these materials. We will discover why in the following sections. Now, let's move on to our other questions about commodities.

Why are commodities an asset that we should be concerned with? As mentioned above, commodities are used in nearly every segment of our everyday lives. Any company that produces a good uses commodities as an input material. All of the food we eat comes from commodities. Commodities are not only used in the obvious ways—you know, we

eat an ear of corn, so the corn is the commodity.
No, there are several other commodities that went
in to producing that ear of corn, such as the fuel
that ran the tractors and the trucks that shipped
the corn, the metal that went into making the
tractor and truck, the water that went into growing
the corn, the minerals that went into the fertilizer
that helped grow the corn.

Imagine all of these commodities and more that
went into producing just one ear of corn. Imagine
how many commodities you use on a daily basis
that you probably are not even aware of. Virtually
everything we do uses some commodity in one
form or another. If commodities are this important
in our daily lives, don't you think it is something we
should consider for our investment portfolios?

So, what makes these materials so valuable, and
what makes us think we can make money by
investing in them? To answer this, we need to look
back at some of the things we talked about before
in our economics section. Since there is a finite
amount of commodities that are available at any
one time on Earth, their value is subject to the law
of supply and demand. This basically says that the
price rises as the demand for a good rises, until
more supply is added to the market. So, if there is
not a large amount of a good available and a lot
of people need it to survive, then the price will go

up. There is another factor here that most people overlook or try to ignore. The number of people who need the material is a factor in the demand and the price of the good, but so is the amount of currency available in the world that can be used to purchase that material.

Obviously, the more people that need it, the more demand there is for that good. As we said above, if there is a fixed supply of that good, then the price of it will go up, as more people try to buy it.

According to the U.S. Census Bureau, the world population has grown from approximately 2.6 billion people in 1950 to approximately 6.8 billion people in 2010.[2] That is an amazing number of people added to the world population in just sixty years. That number is projected to grow to 9 billion people by 2045. As you can see, there are far more people chasing a finite amount of goods than there were just a few years ago. This is surely going to have an effect on the demand for commodities.

World Population: 1950-2050

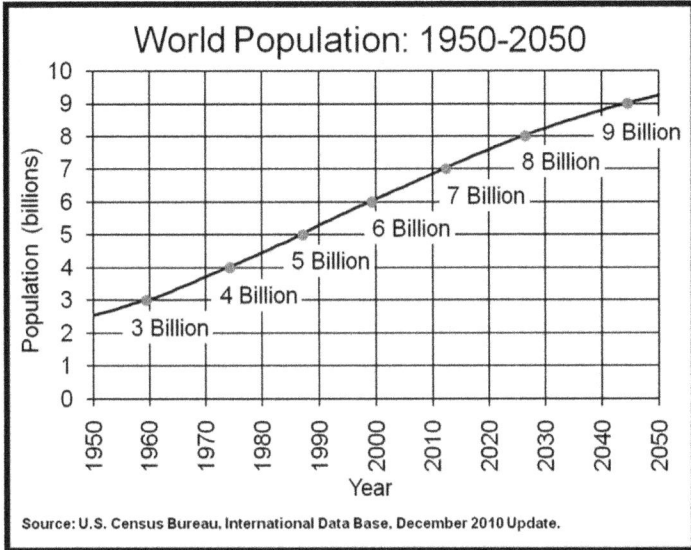

Source: U.S. Census Bureau, International Data Base, December 2010 Update.

The part of the equation that is often overlooked is the amount of money available to buy that good. As governments around the world print more money, there is more money to spend on these materials.

Let's look at it another way. If we are looking at the money as the good that everyone wants, and the government keeps printing more and more of it, then it becomes easily available. At some point, there is even too much of it available. This makes the money worth less, as more and more of it is printed.

So, if we are trading something that becomes worth less and less each day for something that is needed by more and more people, then that item becomes worth more and more in money terms. It takes more and more money to purchase that item, as the money becomes worth less and less. This is the situation we are facing today. As we noted in our economics section, governments around the world are going into more and more debt. To do this, they are printing more and more money to help pay for those debts. Although we know that they can never print enough money to pay off their debts, the quantity of money that they are printing is causing the purchasing power of that money to decline rapidly.

According to the U.S. Federal Reserve, the total amount of money in circulation, widely referred to as the M2 money supply by economists, was $1.1 trillion in February 1980. It was reported at $7.0 trillion in 2011.[3] In thirty years, the money supply increased by $5.9 trillion! Back in February 1960, the total money in circulation was only $159 billion.

As you can see, the amount of money pumped into existence in the last thirty years is causing the dollar to lose nearly all of its purchasing power. What kind of effect do you think this is going to have on commodity prices? They will surely increase in price, as the population and money supply continue to grow.

Now that we know about the demand of commodities increasing and the value of the money used to purchase commodities decreasing, what about the supply of the commodities themselves? Surely we would produce more if there was so much money to be made, right? Well, let's take a look at that.

First, we have to factor government influence in the production of commodities. Governments have recently been limiting the production of commodities through environmental taxes and penalties. As we become more and more concerned about environmental issues, the more difficult it is going to be to produce commodities.

Second, people have lost a desire to make careers out of commodity-related fields. For instance, as of 2007, the average age of the American farmer was fifty-seven years old.[4] This means that they are all nearing retirement, and there is not a new group of farmers coming along behind them. This will surely reduce supply in the coming years as these farmers retire.

Last, it takes many years to increase commodity production. In the case of mining for materials, companies must execute geological surveys, get permits from government agencies, purchase equipment, and hire workers. In the case of agriculture, farmers must purchase the land, prepare the land, plant the crops, harvest the crops, and get them to market. It takes many years to get this production up and running.

With so many factors working against the increase in supply of commodities, investors can feel comfortable that they will not see a huge increase in commodities sold in the market place anytime soon. At this point, we should have a pretty clear picture of the factors that contribute to the increase in commodity prices over the long term. Let's explore some of the other questions we posed at the beginning of this chapter.

So, why do the financial media never talk about commodities and why do very few financial advisors instruct their clients to invest in them? There are several reasons. The first is that it is very difficult to talk about commodity prices rising, without talking about the underlying reasons that they are rising. It is also difficult for the media to encourage investment in commodities because to do so would drive more investment money into this asset class, which would cause prices to rise further. This would be painful for the companies that the financial media are constantly pushing us to buy and sell.

If the financial media were to encourage investment in commodities and contribute to the prices increasing, the companies whose stocks they review would have to pay more for the materials they use to produce the goods they sell. This would cause earnings to be lower, which would cause stock prices to fall.

Another reason financial media never talk about commodities is because the government measures the inflation rate in the country each month. They base a lot of their borrowing and social program payment increases on this inflation rate. For example, social security payments are tied to the Consumer Price Index. This is the main index that the Bureau of Labor Statistics uses to measure inflation. If the CPI goes up, then the amount that the government owes retirees goes up. So the government has an incentive to keep commodity prices down.

So, why have financial advisors not encouraged their clients to purchase commodities? Well, this answer is a little less complicated. Basically, the reason that financial advisors have not encouraged the purchase of commodities is that they generally don't understand them. Until recently, there was no easy way for the average investor to buy into commodities. Investment in commodities used to require that the investor was able to trade directly with the commodity exchange. This was not possible for most people. Because it was not possible for their clients to invest in them, there was no need to learn about commodities

Also, it was expensive to trade with the exchange. In order to buy contracts of commodities from the exchange, you had to buy very large amounts of the commodity. This required investors to make large down payments for the contract. If those contracts went down in value, investors could be on the hook for huge sums. We won't go into all of the details, just know that it was very difficult and risky for most people to invest in commodities until recently.

So, what changed to make them more accessible? The invention of Exchange Traded Funds (ETF) enabled average investors to buy into commodities as they would stocks. The ETF can be made up of many different things. There are now hundreds of ETF investments available in all kinds of areas. Obviously, the area we want to focus on is commodities.

So, which ETFs should we buy and how much of each one? There are many to choose from, but I won't go into specific ones here. You can choose ETFs that reflect one particular commodity, or you can choose ETFs that hold many different commodities so that you can get exposure to many different commodities in one investment.

How much of our total investment should be invested in commodities? Since we have a maximum of 60 percent of our total investment in value stocks, we will invest 20 percent in commodities. This will give us good exposure to commodities without being overloaded. This will also leave us 10 percent of our investment money to invest in precious metals. This amount of exposure allows us to gain from the long-term rise in commodities without being affected too much by the inevitable swings in commodity prices along the way.

We should see the trends of rising prices continue, as the global population and the total amount of money in circulation increase. Prices will fluctuate over the years, as money moves into commodities, but we can be comfortable knowing that the major trends of the world will work in our favor.

Main points from this chapter:

- Commodities are the basic materials that are used every day in the majority of the items we use and consume.
- The law of supply and demand determines the price of commodities.
- The rising demand and prices paid for commodities are determined in large part by the increasing world population and the ever-expanding supply of money.
- Supply is restricted by government regulations on production of commodities, the time it takes to increase production, and the small number of people who devote their careers to commodity production.

- The financial media don't talk about commodities because they do not want to encourage investment, which would increase the price of these materials.
- Companies do not want to see commodity prices increase, because that means their input costs will increase, which affects earnings and reduces stock prices.
- The media do not want to encourage increased prices of commodities, because government inflation measurements are tied to commodity prices.
- Increases in inflation measurements result in increased costs for governments in the area of social benefits.
- Financial advisors did not typically recommend commodity investments in the past, because they were not familiar with them, because commodities were too difficult and risky for the average investor.
- The invention of the Exchange Traded Fund (ETF) has opened up the world of commodities to the average investor.
- We should put 20 percent of our total investment funds into commodity-related ETF investments.

Chapter 7

~ SILVER AND GOLD ~

Very few assets draw the emotional response that silver and gold do. Fans of silver and gold even have a nickname to describe themselves—gold bugs. Those who believe that we should go back to some form of gold- and silver-backed currency are often painted as quacks, cooks, and crazies. Discussion of these precious metals as money draws venomous arguments from both sides.

So, how should we view this subject? Are these metals good investments? What does the historical record say about gold and silver as investments? We will explore these issues in this chapter.

The issue of gold and silver as money is very interesting to say the least. It is likely that both sides of the argument have it wrong. The currency side says that gold and silver are relics and cannot serve as money in today's modern world, where electronic currency digitally flies around the world. The gold and silver side says that currency is worthless money that is backed by nothing and therefore has no value.

Even some of today's most famous financial advisors are on the radio and television every day telling the world why gold is a terrible investment or why gold and silver are the only true protection against currency collapse. This is really a shame, because it causes confusion, and the average investor cannot figure out who is right. Both sides seem to make compelling arguments.

Let's assume that the arguments of both sides are correct in some ways and incorrect in other ways. In what ways are the currency fans correct? In what ways are they wrong? In what ways are the gold bugs correct? In what ways are they wrong?

To determine the facts of gold and silver, we must look back at the history of money in the United States. What is the history of gold as money in the United States? What has happened to the purchasing power of the dollar over time? What effect did the introduction of income taxes and the Federal Reserve have on the incomes and the purchasing power of the average household, over time? Thankfully, most of this history has been captured and provided for us.

I have tracked some statistics and created the following chart in order to show the change in several key metrics. This chart compares the change in the price of silver, the change in the price of gold, the change in the Dow Jones Industrial Average, the US Debt, the rising cost of an item that cost $1.00 in 1970, and the rise of the average household income. These metrics paint a pretty clear picture that, over time, we are losing our purchasing power.

Let's take a look at each item one by one. Then we will compare them to see what they tell us. Hopefully, we can see when we are done with our discussion that gold and silver have done the best job of preserving or even increasing our purchasing power, over time.

That is the real issue that both groups arguing for and against gold and silver are missing. Gold and silver should not be viewed as money that will be used as currency in the future. That is just not possible in today's world economy. It should be used as a store of purchasing power. The data shows that gold and silver have been the best sources for retaining purchasing power, since President Nixon eliminated the gold backing of the dollar in 1971.

Year	Silver Price US$/ozt	Gold Price US$/ozt	Dow Jones Industrial Average	US Debt ($billion)	Price of $1.00 (1970) Item	Average Household Income
1970	$1.63	$35.00	839	370	$1.00	$9,870
1980	$16.39	$612.00	964	908	$2.12	$21,020
1990	$4.06	$383.00	2,634	3,233	$3.37	$29,943
2000	$4.95	$279.00	10,787	5,662	$4.44	$42,148
2010	$20.19	$1,225.00	11,578	14,025	$5.62	$49,777*
3/30/2011	$37.35	$1,419.30	12,377	14,250	$5.70	-
Total % Change	2291.41%	4055.14%	1475.21%	3851.35%	570.00%	504.33%

* Reported for end of 2009

As you can see from the table, if you had taken $10,000 and buried it in your back yard in 1970, it would be worth about $1,754 today. Put another way, you could buy only 17.5% as much stuff today with that money as you could in 1970. That is an 82.5% loss in the value of your money.

If we go back to 1913, when the Federal Reserve was created, it looks even worse. As of June 2009, the dollar was only worth 4.6¢ when compared to what it was worth in 1913. This loss in purchasing power is a silent tax that most people don't even realize they are paying. That is because it happens gradually, over time.

You can see that the loss in purchasing power is hurting the government, too. Our national debt is up 38.5 times what it was in 1970. The government can't keep up with the loss in purchasing power of the dollar. As I pointed out in the chapter on economics, this is becoming apparent to bond investors, as they have stopped buying the government's debt.

So, what is the good news? The good news is that three investments have maintained and even increased your purchasing power over the same time period. Those three investments are the Dow Jones Industrial Average, silver, and gold.

The Dow Jones is up 14.75 times what it was in 1970. This does not include dividends that could have been reinvested for further gains. This also takes into account the massive fall we have seen since the peak in 2007. While the stock market has bounced back quite a bit since it hit bottom a couple of years ago, it still is not back to its peak. There are still two better investments that have returned more on an initial investment made back in 1970.

The first one is silver. Silver is up 22.91 times what its price was in 1970. This is a fantastic return. That means that $10,000 invested in 1970 would now be $229,100. Now we have to reduce it back down to account for the purchasing power that we lost in the dollar of that time period. Reducing that $229,100 by the 82.5 percent in lost purchasing power still leaves us with $40,184 in 1970 purchasing power. So, not only have you retained all of your purchasing power, you have increased it four-fold. Not bad at all. Also, as we will discuss later in this chapter, silver likely has a much brighter future than gold over the next few years.

The last investment on the list is gold. Gold has made an amazing run over the last forty years. It has out gained every other asset class by a long shot. Gold is up 40.55 times its 1970 price. That means that $10,000 invested in gold in 1970 would be $405,500 today. As we did with silver, we need to reduce that number to figure out our purchasing power in 1970 dollars. When we reduce $405,000 by 82.5 percent, we get $71,125. So we increased our purchasing power by over seven-fold. That is an amazing return!

As you can see, gold is our best bet for retaining our purchasing power, as our dollar will continue to be devalued in the future. Silver comes in second. Investing in the Dow Jones comes in third.

One short note, you might be asking yourself, "Why don't I just invest everything in gold, and forget everything else?" That is a good question, but you have to understand that investing in value stocks has outpaced even the returns of gold over time. Plus, we want to diversify our portfolio, so that we never get caught in a bad position if one investment takes a downturn.

So, now, the question becomes, "That is great that gold has gone up so much over the last forty years, but do you think it can keep going up?" The answer to that question in a word is—yes! As we discussed in the economics chapter, the governments of the west are reaching the point of no return when it comes to their debt. As we mentioned earlier, investors all over the world recognize that government debt is no longer a safe investment. Since there are trillions of dollars that will need to be invested, and they are not going to go into government debt, where are they going to go? Gold, silver, commodities, and stocks are the places where we believe this money will flow.

Gold and silver are going to be recipients of a lot of this money because, as we mentioned before, money flows to where it is treated best. Most people in the world generally view gold and silver as safe places to invest money. In the U.S., we have an aversion to gold and silver, because we have been told that they are to be used for jewelry and not for investment.

Another reason that the average U.S. citizen does not view gold and silver as investments is because, like commodities, there has historically been no easy way to invest in these metals. In the past, you could buy gold and silver jewelry, but trying to sell it was a tough thing to do. After paying a marked-up price to a jeweler when he bought the metal, the average citizen would then traditionally only be able to sell his metal to a pawn shop where he would typically get a low-ball offer.

Of course, there were coin shops that the metal investor could deal with, but this practice was viewed as collecting, which very few people did. People often viewed collecting coins as a hobby like collecting baseball cards or stamps. These stigmas and issues are no longer a problem for the investor who wants to put his or her money in gold or silver.

Like commodities, investing in precious metals has become more popular with the invention of exchange-traded funds. There are several ETFs available now that hold gold and silver. Some of them hold gold and silver contracts, and some of them hold the physical gold and silver in vaults. This is important if you ever want to cash in your shares for physical metal, but if you want to hold the physical metal, you should probably just buy bullion to begin with.

Now that these ETFs are available for investors who want to put some of their money in precious metals, it is easier than ever to become a precious metals investor. Once the average U.S. citizen figures out that gold and silver are two of the safest investments out there, the money should flow into these metals.

So how much of our portfolio should go into these precious metals and which one should we put the majority of our investment money into? First off, 20 percent is the amount of money that we should be allocating to precious metals. A lot of financial advisors say to max out at 10 percent, but considering the performance of gold and silver over the last forty years, 10 percent seems too low.

As for which metal should get the majority of our precious metals money, the answer is silver. While gold has had a great run over the last forty years and should keep moving up, based on all of the factors we have previously listed, silver likely has more upside.

First, silver is cheaper, so you can buy more of it. Would you rather own forty ounces of silver or one ounce of gold? Also, on a percentage basis, silver can move up faster than gold can. To move up 10 percent, silver only has to increase in price by $3.75, whereas gold has to increase in price by $142. Now these are not fundamental reasons to buy silver over gold, they are just the practical reasons.

One of the biggest reasons to buy silver over gold has to do with how much of each metal is available and how each metal is used. Gold is typically mined and held as a store of value, so most of the gold ever mined is still in existence.

Silver, on the other hand, is used in industrial applications, such as medical equipment, mirrors, optical equipment, dental fillings, electronics, photography, and even clothing. Due to this widespread industrial use of silver, the majority of the silver that has been mined has been consumed in these industrial applications.

According to estimates by the World Gold Council and the Silver Institute, there is approximately seven times more gold above ground than there is silver, today. Because of its relative scarcity and its many industrial uses, silver is poised to advance in price very dramatically over the coming years.

Whether you ultimately decide to purchase gold or silver, physical metal or ETFs, the case has been made that these metals are sure to provide a reliable store of your purchasing power over the coming years. Don't let the money versus non-money advocates out there sway you. Gold and silver are very valuable, not as exchangeable money, but as protectors of purchasing power.

Main points from this chapter:

- Gold and silver should be viewed as a store of purchasing power, not money to be used in exchange.
- The dollar has lost 82.5 percent of its purchasing power since 1970.
- Average household income has increased five-fold since 1970 and still hasn't kept up with the falling dollar.
- U.S. government debt has increased 38.5 times since 1970.
- The Dow Jones has increased 14.75 times since 1970.
- Silver has increased 22.91 times since 1970.
- Gold has led the way, increasing 40.55 times since 1970.
- As money flows out of government debt, it should flow into stocks, commodities, and precious metals
- Exchange Traded Funds have made it much easier for the average investor to invest in gold and silver.
- We should put 20 percent of our portfolio into gold and silver, with the larger portion of that money going to silver.
- Silver is much cheaper than gold, so it can increase on a percentage basis much easier, and you can buy more ounces of it

- Due to silver's wide range of industrial uses, leading precious metals research organizations estimate that there is currently seven times more gold than silver available for investment in the world.

Chapter 8

~ BONDS ~

A lot of people prefer the safety of investing their money in government debt—U.S. Treasury Bonds or Municipal Bonds. Some people also like to invest in Corporate Bonds. In this chapter, we are going to learn that, not only are these investments not safe, but they could be the most dangerous of all outside of speculation. We will learn what debt actually is in practical terms, and why most debt will never be repaid.

Purchasing debt—government debt or any other kind—is actually just the process of lending money to someone. A bond is really just a promise to pay back debt that is owed to the bondholder. So, when you own a bond, you own nothing more than a promise. It is really no different than the note on your car or the mortgage on your house, except for one key point. If you fail to repay the note on your car or the mortgage on your house, the bank has something they can repossess—your car or house. If the government fails to repay you for the bond that you hold, there is nothing you can claim against that bond. You simply lose all of your investment.

If a bond is really just a promise to repay a debt, the key question should then become, "Where is the money going to come from to repay the money that I loaned the debtor?" Unfortunately, this is not the question that people ask themselves when they purchase bonds. They typically ask themselves how much interest they are going to earn or how long until the bond matures.

Other key questions that should be asked are these: To whom else does this debtor owe money? and How much total debt does this debtor have? These are the exact questions that a bank would want to know when deciding whether or not to lend you money. Unfortunately, when the average investor is deciding whether or not to purchase bonds, he or she rarely asks these questions.

Answering these questions for corporate debtors can get tricky, so we will explore those answers a little later in the chapter. For now, let's try to answer the three main questions, as they pertain to government debt. We will start with Federal government debt.

So, where is the Federal Government going to get the money to repay their debts? According to figures from Whitehouse.gov[5], total tax receipts for 2010 were $2.16 trillion against a budget of $3.46 trillion. This resulted in a deficit of $1.29 trillion. That deficit is the portion that is funded by government debt.

To put this in a different perspective, just to finance one year's worth of expenses, the Federal Government had to use debt to fund 37.3 percent of its budget. The picture gets even worse in 2011 with over 43 percent of annual expenses expected to be funded by debt. This comes from the White House's own projections!

So the Federal Government is living year-to-year on debt. They cannot even pay their annual bills with taxpayer money. How do you think they are ever going to be able to pay off their debts?

So, how much total debt does the Federal Government have to repay? In other words, how much does the Federal Government owe their creditors? According to Treasurydirect.gov[6], the Federal Government owes $14.27 trillion as of March 31, 2011. This is just the current outstanding debt. This does not include unfunded liabilities, such as future Social Security, Welfare, and Medicare payments. This also does not include the liabilities of Fannie Mae and Freddie Mac. These unfunded liabilities have been estimated to be from $50 trillion to $70 trillion, depending on the source. For now, we will just focus on the $14.27 trillion of current liabilities.

According to Treasurydirect.gov[7], the interest paid on the national debt in 2010 was $413.95 billion. This represents 11.96 percent of the annual budget. The point here is that our government is deep in debt. Even the interest that we pay each year is beginning to take up a sizeable portion of annual budget.

So, who owns all of this Federal debt? The largest foreign holders of our debt, according to the latest treasury report, in January 2011[8], are China with $1.115 trillion, Japan with $886 billion, United Kingdom with $278 billion, and the oil producing nations of the Middle East with $215.5 billion. The total value of the U.S. government debt owned by foreign owners is $4.37 trillion, as of December 2010[9].

Who else owns the Federal debt if foreign ownership only accounts for 31.15 percent of it? As of December 2010[9] $5.656 trillion is owned by the Federal Reserve and intra-governmental accounts. This accounts for 40.3 percent of the total Federal debt. The remaining 28.5 percent, or $3.999 trillion, is owned by private investors[9].

These ratios are sure to change over the coming months, as private investors sell their Treasury Securities (Federal debt), as fast as they possibly can. The largest bond fund in the world recently announced that they had completely sold all of their Treasury Securities as of March 2011.

As mentioned previously in the economics chapter, the Federal Reserve has recently had to step in to buy 70 percent of the Treasury Securities offered in recent months. This is surely a sign that no one else wants to purchase U.S. government debt anymore. So if no one else wants to buy it, why should you hold it in your portfolio?

People continue to say in the media that the U.S. government has never had a financial default in its history. This is simply not true. As a matter of fact, the U.S. government defaulted on its financial obligations in 1971, when President Nixon took us off of the gold standard. He made this move because other countries wanted to redeem their dollars for gold, and we simply did not have the gold to give them. The U.S. government has defaulted on its financial obligations before, and it will most likely do it again. Do you really want to be holding Federal debt when it happens?

Now, let's talk about municipal debt—debt owed by state and local governments. This situation is worse than the Federal debt situation. At least the Federal government can keep devaluing the dollar by selling Treasury Securities to the Federal Reserve, in exchange for more and more dollars created out of thin air. The State and Local governments cannot print money to exchange for their debt securities. These governments actually have to pay them back or default on the debt by declaring bankruptcy.

Many people like to purchase these bonds because of their historically-low default rates and their tax-exempt status. The problem is that most of the state and local governments are running out of money. There has already been legislation proposed in several states, which would allow states and local governments to declare bankruptcy and default on their debt obligations. This is being considered, because state and local governments can only get money in two ways: by issuing debt and collecting taxes.

For decades, these state governments have relied on debt and taxes to fund unneeded projects, hire too many workers, and provide unneeded services. A lot of the taxes that these governments relied upon were property taxes, which have taken a huge hit in recent years, with the collapse of the real estate market. As house prices have declined, so have the tax dollars collected on those houses. This has hurt governments that had already spent too much money and were now going to be collecting less money than they budgeted.

I am sure that there are some local government bonds that are safe to invest in, but finding them is like finding a needle in a haystack. There are no state governments that I would feel comfortable loaning money to. With this in mind, and the fact that tax revenues are declining all across the country, as people lose their jobs and their homes, why would we loan money to state and local governments who are even less likely to pay us back than the Federal government?

That leaves us with corporate debt. These bonds are typically rated from AAA all the way down to NR. An AAA rating is supposed to mean that these are the safest bonds available, and that there is virtually no risk of default. The NR rating is supposed to mean that the company is virtually certain to default on those bonds.

While we certainly want to stay away from any bonds rated lower than AAA, we cannot be completely comfortable with AAA bonds, either. As shown in the housing collapse, some bonds that were rated AAA collapsed, as the companies that owed the debts went bankrupt. The ratings agencies don't always have the correct incentives to give accurate ratings for these bonds, but that is another subject that could fill up a whole other book.

Suffice it to say that we need to be careful if we choose to select any corporate bonds. While there are really no bonds that should be included in our portfolio, if you absolutely must own some bonds in your portfolio, AAA corporate bonds are the only ones you should consider. When we start to look at these AAA rated corporate bonds, we need to consider the three questions that we listed above:

- How is this company going to make the money to pay me back?
- How much money does this company owe already?
- To whom does this company owe money?

If you can answer all of those questions and feel comfortable that the company is stable enough to pay you back, then you can consider purchasing some of their bonds.

As a word of warning, however, there are other things that need to be considered when deciding to purchase corporate bonds. Some of these additional issues are:

- If the company defaults, are these notes secured by any of the company's property?
- Are there any other bonds that would be listed ahead of my bonds for recovering their investment in the event of a default?
- Are these bonds convertible into stock or some other security?
- Can the company repurchase the bonds from me at an earlier date than the maturity date, without penalty?

If you cannot answer these questions, or you are not sure where to even look for the answers to these questions, stay away from corporate bonds. While they can be safer than U.S. Treasury or municipal debt, they are also much more complicated.

As a last point of interest, let's look at the current rates of interest that the three different types are paying investors. Below is a chart that captures the rates of interest for the three different types of debt at different maturity dates, as of April 2, 2011.

Bond Yields 4/2/11			
	US Treasury	Municpal AAA	Corporate AAA
2 Year	0.82	0.63	1.27*
5 Year	2.26	1.64	2.45
10 Year	3.44	2.95	3.98
20 Year	-	4.62	5.35
30 Year	4.48	-	-

Source: Yahoo! Finance
*2 Year Corporate AA

As you can see from the chart, corporate debt typically has the highest interest rates, followed by U.S. Treasury (Federal) debt, and then municipal debt. None of these types of debt are currently paying anything near what should be considered an acceptable rate of interest, considering the risk that they are asking you to take. Do you think a bank would give someone a loan for ten years at 3 percent to 4 percent interest, if they were very likely to default on that loan? Of course they wouldn't, so why should you be any different? You shouldn't be any different. Loaning money to a government, especially in today's economic environment, is a sucker's game.

Main points from this chapter:

- Purchasing debt is just lending to the debt issuer.
- A bond is just a promise to pay back the debt represented by the bond.
- A lender should always ask three questions before lending money:
  1. Where is the money going to come form to repay the debt?
  2. How much debt does the borrower owe?
  3. To whom does the borrower owe money?
- The Federal government currently has $14.25 trillion in outstanding debt.
- In 2010, the Federal budget was funded 63 percent with taxes and 37 percent with new debt.
- In 2010, 11.96 percent of the annual budget was used to pay the interest on the outstanding debt.
- In 2011, the Federal budget is projected to be funded 57 percent with taxes and 43 percent with new debt.
- Of the $14.25 trillion owed, 31.15 percent is owned by foreigners, 40.3 percent is owned

by the Federal Reserve, and 28.5 percent is owned by private investors.

- The Federal Reserve had to dramatically increase purchases of U.S. Treasury debt in recent months, as private investors had not only stopped buying these securities, but had been massively selling them.

- The U.S. government defaulted on financial obligations in the past when President Nixon removed the dollar from the gold standard.

- The municipal debt situation is actually worse than the Federal situation, because municipal governments cannot print new money to help pay for their debts.

- Several states have proposed legislation that would allow local governments and states to declare bankruptcy and default on their debts.

- Many state and local governments are struggling to repay debts, because their tax revenue has dramatically fallen, as unemployment has risen and the housing market has crashed.

- Corporate debt is even trickier than government debt, because you have to take other factors into consideration:

  1. Are the bonds secured by any of the company's assets?

2. Are there any other bonds ahead of my bonds or creditors in the debt structure?
3. Are the bonds convertible into stock or other types of securities?
4. Can the company repay the bonds early without penalty?

- If you absolutely have to own bonds, AAA rated corporate bonds are probably the best ones to own.
- None of the three types of debt are paying interest rates, considered as an acceptable rate of interest to compensate for the risk the lender is taking on.

Chapter 9

~ SPECULATION ~

Now we get to the subject no one likes to talk
about. As I mentioned in the beginning of this
book, investing is to be viewed as a long-term
ownership interest in a company or asset. Anything
else is *speculation*.

So what is wrong with speculation? From a moral
or ethical perspective, there is nothing wrong with
it. There is nothing wrong with it if you can put in
the time to master it. The problem is that the vast
majority of the people reading this book do not
have the time or the resources to be speculators.

If we know that speculation is not investing, what
exactly is it? Speculation is actually a very broad
label that should be applied to what most people
refer to as *investing* today. Instead, speculation is
essentially gambling.

This is exactly why Wall Street continues to
advocate that you make short-term trades. This is
why they constantly barrage you with financial news

about stock prices, earnings reports, and any other tiny piece of information they can use to spin some story about why a stock is going to go up or down in price.

This is just like, when you go to a casino and they have flashing lights and sounds buzzing all around you, it pulls you into everything that is going on. It makes you want to do something. You need to place a bet or make a trade. You need to do something. The last thing they want you to do is invest for the long term.

Some people may say, "Well there are people who make money in casinos." Yes there are. They are called professional gamblers. There are people who make money speculating in the market, too. They are called professional traders. They typically have a lot of money they can trade each day, and they pay much smaller trading fees on a percentage basis than you and I have to pay.

This means that they can trade stocks and take very small percentage gains each day to earn a living. They have multiple millions of dollars that they are trading, so making a profit is much easier for them than it is for you and me.

I understand your desire to want to try new methods to make a quick buck. Every day there seems to be some new method that is guaranteed

to make you untold riches by trading in the market.
I have fallen pray to all of them, myself, it seems.
I have tried method after method of speculation,
attempting to get rich in the markets. It is very
difficult, to say the least!

Let's take a few minutes to look at some of the
methods of speculation that are popular today. We
will look at the promise of each one, and then look
at the drawbacks for each method. I know some
people will still want to speculate, because we all
have the itch to gamble on some level. Because
of this, at the end of the chapter, we will lay out a
plan that will allow you to use part of your portfolio
for speculation, without putting too much of your
portfolio at risk.

The first strategy we will address is buying the
stock of distressed companies. Oftentimes,
companies will fall into dire straights for one
reason or another. Maybe their CEO was
embezzling money from the company, or maybe
they are in an industry that is dying. Whatever the
reason, the stock is trading at a very low price—
often below $1.

The thinking here is that, if you can buy the shares
very cheap, and the company can turn the situation
around, then you can make a ton of money. It
is true that there is a slight possibility this could
happen. I have even done it a few times. Let me tell

you, though, I have been burned many more times than I have won.

With this strategy, there are many parts that move behind the scenes. What if the company declares bankruptcy? You could lose all of your investment. It is best to just stay away from distressed companies. This is not a safe place to put your money.

The next strategy we want to talk about is high-growth or momentum stocks. These are the stocks that are all over the financial news. These are the stocks that everyone loves to talk about. These are the cool stocks. You know the ones in high school that everyone wanted to be friends with? These are the stocks that I am talking about.

Sometimes, these stocks are legitimate companies that can make you rich, but most times they are just fads that will make you poor. For every Microsoft or Wal-Mart, there are ten fad companies. Companies that have a fad product that everyone loves for a minute, then they crash like a stone, when the public moves on to the next cool thing.

It is true that, sometimes, you come across an Apple type of company that will make you rich, if you just close your eyes and hope that they continue coming out with products that everyone just has to have. The problem is that none of us can tell the future, so none of us knows if our popular company will continue to be popular into the future.

We can all look around and find companies that were the big thing in their day, that are now closed down or close to it. Take textile companies for example. In their day, everyone wanted to own textile stocks. Now, all of the textile production has been shipped overseas. At their peak, no one could have told you that none of those companies would be here in ten or twenty years.

Other classic recent examples are the high fliers of the late 1990s with the tech bubble. It seemed like every dotcom company out there was moving up in price. It seemed like buying and owning those stocks was a sure path to riches. Where did that end up? Most of those companies are no longer with us, and their stockholders lost their entire investment.

I could go on and on about momentum stocks that everyone loved and got burned by. Remember we are investing for the long term. That inherently makes us go against the crowd. While everyone else is gambling on the day's current high-flier, we will be looking for value.

Another speculation strategy is to buy the very low-priced stock of companies that we suspect may have some reason to dramatically increase in price at a later date. An example is a company that is working on technology that could run a car on water. The stock might be trading at a very low price, because everyone sees it as a low probability that the technology will ever be completed.

The penny stock universe is littered with these types of companies. They promise great things, but have never shown any real products. Buying the stock is really a gamble on whether they can actually do what they claim they can do.

Another example is oil exploration or precious metals mining companies who own mineral rights to land that is suspected to have valuable resources under it. The stock is trading cheaply, because the resources have not been proven, and they still have to pull them out of the ground.

Even if the resource is proven, the companies still have to go through all of the government red tape and the scaling up of production, as we mentioned back in the commodities chapter. It could be years before these companies actually make any money, if they ever do.

Another, more sophisticated strategy is trading derivatives, such as options. Options are essentially contracts to buy or sell a stock at a certain price on a certain date. You make money by betting that the price of the stock will be higher than the level of the option you bought. For example, suppose I buy an option to buy one hundred shares of XYC Corporation on June 30, 2011 for $20 per share. When June 30, 2011 comes around, let's say the share price is $25. That means for those one hundred shares, I would make $5 per share, minus the price I paid for the option itself.

Options are inherently speculative by their very nature. Not only are they not tied directly to the performance of the company, they can expire. If the price of the stock in the example above closed at $19 per share on June 30, 2011, my options would have expired and would be worthless. I would have lost all of the money I used to purchase the options. I have been here before, and it is painful to watch your money just disappear, as if it never existed.

Another very popular form of speculation is called technical analysis. This is the practice of using some sort of mechanical indicator to tell you when to buy or sell a stock. This strategy works by watching the stock and other indicators that have been invented over time, which supposedly indicate that the price is going to keep going up for a while, or is going to go down for a while. I was a huge fan of this strategy, when I was first started learning about investing in stocks. I learned, after many unsuccessful attempts at making money, that this strategy does not typically work, either.

Now there are technical-analysis strategies that I can personally say do work, but they require a large amount of money and an ability to commit all of your time to tracking the price movements of the stock that you are trading. Most of us do not have the time, nor do we have the resources to sit and track stock prices all day long.

As an aside, if you do have the resources and time to commit to a technical analysis strategy, check out Richard Dennis and his Turtle Trader experiment[10]. He proved that he could make successful traders out of anyone who would follow his rules, no matter what, had ample resources to trade with, was trading in a market steadily trending up or down, and had the time to sit and track stock prices all day long. I do not recommend this strategy for investment purposes, but I would be remiss if I did not at least let you know of the one technical analysis strategy I have found that actually does work under the right circumstances.

So, we mentioned at the beginning of the chapter that we would lay out a strategy to commit a portion of investment funds to speculation, if we came across some speculative situation that we just could not pass up. Here is the rule: never put more than 10 percent of your total portfolio into speculation. We prefer zero percent in this area, but we can live with 10 percent.

If you have to take the 10 percent to speculate, take 5 percent out of the value-stock portion and 5 percent out of the commodity portion of your portfolio. Again, speculation is never advocated, but we have to be realistic. Because of that, we have to put ground rules in place to keep our wild, speculative sides in check.

Main points from this chapter:

- Speculation is no different than gambling at a casino.
- There are professional traders who make money speculating, just as there are professional gamblers who make money gambling.
- Buying the stock of distressed companies is always a gamble, because there are always things going on behind the scenes that we can never know about: financial issues, accounting scandals, legal issues, or a dying industry.
- Growth stocks are like the cool kids in high school—everyone loves them, until they burn you; for every Microsoft, there are a hundred high fliers that crashed and burned.
- Gambling on stocks with some technology or mineral rights that could pay off big in the future is always a risk; most times, these

companies have never made any money, and their promise is just a dream.

- Trading options is always risky because they eventually expire; nothing that can expire worthless can be called a long-term investment.
- Technical analysis is the definition of speculation; stocks are traded on price indicators, not on the fundamentals of the companies underlying the stocks.
- There is one form of technical analysis that I do know does work in the right situations— Richard Dennis' price breakout strategy (Turtle Trader Experiment); this strategy is still not recommended.
- If you absolutely must speculate on something, never put more than 10 percent of your total portfolio into the speculative trade; we must always protect our investment money for the long term.

Chapter 10

~ PUTTING IT ALL TOGETHER ~

This book has been about laying out a strategy for your whole financial life. It has been about getting your personal finances in order, so that you can learn to invest for your future. The goal was to teach you the strategies that Wall Street and the financial media don't want you to know about, so that you can work your way toward financial freedom.

We have to break away from the strategies and advice that doesn't work. We have to learn to think for ourselves and implement strategies that do work. After all, it is up to you to make sure that your financial health is the best that it can be. No one else cares about your financial health quite as much as you do. Let's review what we have learned.

First we have to make good decisions when it comes to our personal finances. None of us was ever taught how to be savvy with our money. So don't beat yourself up if you are in a position that you don't like concerning your finances.

So, what were the key points that we learned to get our personal finances in order? We want to make sure that we are paying as little interest as possible in all of our transactions. Obviously the best way to do that is to become debt free.

Becoming debt free is a long journey for most of us, so we set up strategies for making decisions on big-ticket items. We set rules in place to determine how much house we could afford, how much car we could afford, and how much of a down payment we should make on each of those items. We then set rules for how long our loan terms should be for each of those items.

We also want to make sure that we never use credit cards, unless it is an absolute emergency. Even then, if you have some other way to pay for the emergency, use the other method. Credit cards are financial suicide.

We also want to consider all of the hidden costs when making decisions, such as going to college/ graduate school or purchasing a car. Oftentimes, the sticker price is only a small portion of the overall cost, and the payback is usually not quite as great as we think it is going to be. Always look for other methods to accomplish your goals, rather than the ones that are going to put you deep into debt.

Always make sure that you are funding your savings and investment accounts as you are paying down your debt. Those accounts are just as important as paying down your debt. Those are the accounts that are going to support you in the future. Make sure that you are funding those accounts in equal proportions—half in your savings, half in your investment account. These accounts will add up fast, if you use this method. It will make you feel much better about your financial health, as you see these accounts build, rather than just seeing your debts shrink. You need to be working on both aspects every day.

Next we talked about economics. This subject is not nearly as complicated as the financial media, politicians, and economists want you to believe it is. Remember that money is just the physical reward for labor and innovation, and it flows like water to places that it is treated best. Right now, the U.S. is not creating a very inviting atmosphere for money to flow to, so it is flowing to other places.

The government debt of western countries, including the U.S., is quickly becoming very unfriendly towards money. As these governments rack up more and more debt, it becomes obvious to everyone that they can never repay that debt. Therefore, money is going to flow to other places in the future.

Where is the money going to flow? It is likely going to flow into commodities, stocks, and precious metals. The countries that are going to receive this inflow of money are likely going to be China, Brazil, Costa Rica, Panama, Chile, and a few others. These countries are creating inviting atmospheres for money.

Since we cannot likely drop everything and move to one of these other countries, how do we position ourselves to gain from the coming change in the flow of money? The first thing we have to understand is that, if we want to be successful with our money, we need to invest it, not speculate with it. Investing means buying into assets with a long-term view of the value increasing in those assets. Speculating is what most financial advisors on Wall Street and the financial media want you to do. They want you to trade often, so that you can rack up trading fees and hand your money over to them. This is not a good strategy for making money over the long term.

So, what do we need to know to be good investors? The first thing we need to know is how to properly value companies. This is actually much easier than it sounds. We just need to know a few things about the company to determine if it is worth investing in—our back-of-the-napkin calculations. To do this, we use the formula that I developed to arrive at one number that will allow us to quickly determine if a stock is cheap or not—Percent of Value (%V). That formula is:

$$\%V = \frac{Price}{Intrinsic\,Value} + \frac{EV\,/\,EBITDA}{10}$$

This formula answers all of the questions about the performance of the company and the state of the company's financial health. The only thing it does not tell you is what kind of business the company operates in. You will have to do a little research to find the answer to that question for each company you look at.

After we calculate the %V using the formula, we rank the stocks from the lowest %V to the highest. We want to buy the stocks with the lowest %V. This indicates that they are priced the lowest versus their value.

So when do we sell the stocks once we buy them? We have four basic rules:

1. The stock rises to 80 percent of its intrinsic value.
2. The stock rises to 1.7 or more %V.
3. The company is bought out and the stock is retired.
4. Something negative changes in the company that affects its performance.

Only after one of these criteria is met do we want to sell one of our stocks. We want to make sure that we give the stock ample time to reflect the true value of the company.

We then moved on to commodities where we noted that the world population is growing at an unprecedented rate, while the world is simultaneously being flooded with money. Also, the world's supply of commodities is dwindling by the day. We may not be close to running out of resources, but we are falling further and further behind the demand for them each year. These three things are creating an environment for the value and price of commodities to rise significantly for the foreseeable future.

We definitely want to have part of our portfolio invested in commodities, if for no other reason than to offset the rising prices that we will be paying for the resources that we consume each day. By investing in commodities, we stand a chance of outpacing our rising prices with the money that we make with our investments. This is not guaranteed, but it is definitely better than if we had no financial interest in commodities at all.

We then moved on to gold and silver, where we discovered that the purchasing power of our dollar has fallen by 82.5 percent since 1970. This is astounding. This means that $10,000 buried in the ground in 1970 would have the same purchasing power today as $1,754 did in 1970. Talk about a silent tax on the people!

We compared this loss in purchasing power to the rise in household incomes and discovered that household incomes have not quite kept up with the loss of our purchasing power. We also compared the U.S. government's debt increase since 1970 and found that it had increased by 38.5 times! This is not good news for us as American citizens.

While comparing the previous three items, we also looked at the performance of gold, silver, and the Dow Jones, without dividends factored in since 1970. This comparison showed us that gold has led the way with a 40.5-fold increase. Silver was second with a 22.9-fold increase. The Dow Jones came in third with a 14.75-fold increase. The clear winner is gold, although all three of these assets outpaced the rate that the dollar fell. You would have come out ahead investing in any of these three and holding your investment since 1970.

This makes a great case for investing in gold and silver, even though neither the financial media nor Wall Street want to recommend it as an investment. We also discovered that silver is actually poised to outperform gold in the coming years, because silver is typically consumed by industrial use, whereas gold is typically hoarded. There is reportedly six to seven times more gold than silver in circulation today.

Investing in bonds was the next topic we covered. As we discussed, government bonds could be one of the worst risk-to-reward investments you could make these days. With the large amount of government debt, and the fact that the federal government is borrowing over 35 percent per year to pay for its budget, there is no way that they will ever be able to pay back the bondholders who own their debt.

Municipal bonds are in even worse shape, because they cannot print money in order to pay the interest on their debt like the federal government can. Another issue for the municipal debtors is that they are seeing shrinking tax revenues due to the high level of unemployment and the collapse of the real estate market. With rising costs and shrinking revenue, they are bound to begin defaulting *en masse*. We have already seen several states propose legislation that would allow local governments to declare bankruptcy and default on their debts. This is a very dangerous position to be in, if you are the one who owns this debt.

Corporate debt, on the other hand, may be safer than government debt, depending on the company and the priority of the particular bonds you buy. The problem with corporate debt is that there are many more factors that you need to take into account, when deciding which corporate bonds to purchase. This is a much more complicated decision-making process than that involved in purchasing government bonds. With that said, if you absolutely must own bonds, make sure that you purchase safe, AAA rated corporate bonds from stable companies.

The last topic we covered was speculation. Remember that speculation is exactly what Wall Street and the financial media want us to engage in. They want us trading on every tip, so that we rack up fees and lose money to them. Speculation is a sucker's game. We went through several different types of speculation and gave reasons for staying away from each of them.

Since speculation is gambling, and most of us have an innate desire to gamble, we allocated 10 percent of our total portfolio for speculation. This 10 percent is to be used only if absolutely necessary. We do not recommend speculating at all. Stay away from it if at all possible. However, if you absolutely must engage in speculation, limit it to 10 percent of the portfolio. This will allow you to limit your losses and keep the bulk of your portfolio on the right track.

The optimal allocation for our investment portfolio should be 60 percent in value stocks, 20 percent in commodities, and 20 percent in gold and silver. This allocation should provide nice returns over the long-term. Stick to this formula, and you should be rewarded.